MW00817191

The
SLOW-COOKER
SAVANT

The
SLOW-COOKER
SAVANT

YOU CAN BE A DINNER HERO 52 WEEKS OF THE YEAR!

STERLING MILLER

MILL CITY **PRESS**

Mill City Press, Inc.
2301 Lucien Way #415
Maitland, FL 32751
407.339.4217
www.millcitypress.net

© 2018 by Sterling Miller

All rights reserved. No part of this publication may be reproduced, stored in a retrieval system, or transmitted, in any form or by any means, electronic, mechanical, photocopying, recording, or otherwise, without the prior written permission of the author.

Printed in the United States of America

ISBN-13: 9781545645376

Table of Contents

Introduction

I have always been fascinated by cooking. Even as a teenager growing up, I would sneak minutes in front of the television and watch Julia Child get hammered on wine and do some French cooking on the local PBS channel. Yep, I was a weird kid. Today, I often watch cooking shows like *Iron Chef* or *Chopped* or *Drive-In, Diners and Dives* to catch a few tips to use at home. For our most recent Christmas my wife and daughters bought me a set of high-end mixing bowls. Now that's love! And, of course, no one touches the grill outside but the grill-*master* himself. But, I wasn't always a good cook. It took me a long time to get to a place where I was truly proud of my ability to put something on the table that people really, really liked. Like most, it started with my mom, Carole, a first-generation Italian-American somehow transported from Brooklyn, New York, to the culinary hot spot of York, Nebraska, where I grew up dining on the fare of the *Chances R*, the *Elks Club*, and, of course, *American Legion Post #19*. Cooking is everything to my mom, her entire day is based around what to eat and when. Yet, while I grew up with a lot of pressure to eat, I didn't really feel any pressure to learn to cook until I left for college.

Just before I left for school my mom showed me a few tricks just in case I would ever have to cook for myself. She also showed me how to wash clothes just in case I was too lazy to drive the 45 miles back home every couple of weeks to have her do it for me. Sadly, both skills were wasted with me living in a dorm the first two years. If the cafeteria wasn't cutting it, my cooking options were limited to Domino's Pizza, my friend Barry Redfern's hot plate, and some weird device I owned called a *Hotdogger* from our good friends at Presto. The *Hotdogger* was a rectangular plastic and metal case with a curved clear plastic lid. Inside, there was a series of 12 metal points (six on each side) unto which you placed the ends of your hotdogs, lining them up in a row of six across. Then you closed the lid, turned on the electricity (which meant plugging it into the wall, as there was no on/off switch), and let it "cook" for about 60 seconds (when you unplugged it). It wasn't pretty. It smelled like Frankenstein's asshole and tasted worse. Unfortunately (?), they do not make the *Hotdogger* any longer as hotdog capital punishment was banned around 1985. Seriously, though, this was a thing. Google it.

Eventually, I did move into an apartment where all my mom's cooking instructions were actually useful. Well, except for one: using a slow-cooker (or, as more often called by its most common brand name, a Crock Pot©). The extent of my mom's teaching here consisted of putting some type of meat (pork chops to be exact) into the slow-cooker, adding a can of mushroom soup, covering it up and turning the knob to "low" for seven hours. What did I get? Some gloppy pork chops smothered in mushroom soup. Let's just say this was not a big favorite or either me or my then roommate Greg – who would literally eat anything. And, long story short, that was the end of my slow-cookery days for a few decades. It also made me resent pork chops for a good while too, which was unfortunate for America's pork producers.

About five years ago, though, I rediscovered the slow-cooker. My wife and I had one (wedding present?) that we had dragged from St. Louis to Dallas many years ago. Around this time, I decided to really learn to cook. At least more than grilling steaks and hamburgers. And there was the slow-cooker staring at me from its perch up high in the pantry, saying "use me, goddamit!" – which was weird since most days you don't expect profanity from a small kitchen appliance. Fortunately, around this time slow-cooker technology finally caught up with the 21st century. Actually, that is not correct. Slow-cooker technology was - and is - exactly the same as it was 50 years ago. What changed was people realizing that the slow-cooker is not just a "dump and go" way to cook. If you spend the right amount of time on the *preparation* of the ingredients, you can cook up some excellent food – way better than the gloppy pork chops that haunt me still (though you can make those if you want too). My epiphany came during a visit to Santa Fe, New Mexico and a bowl of Green Chile

Posole. I wanted to make this for myself at home but was at a loss as to how to do it. By chance I came across a recipe for it that called for a slow-cooker. Hey, I have one of those! I didn't make it exactly as described in the recipe, but it turned out so well that my wife and daughters asked for me to try something else. So, I made a slow-cooker pot roast (the Dane Cook of slow-cooker meals). Not only was the aroma of the cooking roast wafting through the house for hours phenomenal, they loved it. Dad was a dinner superhero! I was hooked, and my slow-cooker odyssey began in earnest.

Over the last five years I have tried a number of different recipes in the slow-cooker. While I have had a few "right-in-the-trash-can" epic fails, most turned out great, some even awesome. Which is the beauty of the slow-cooker, i.e., it is really hard to mess it up. Some recipes in this book are from my mom, some I created on my own, and a lot are my own adaptations of recipes people have given me to try or I have otherwise found. And that is the other beautiful thing about slow-cookers: experimentation is highly encouraged! In fact, I fully expect that each of you will take the recipes in this book and make them your own (just be sure to pay for the book, okay?).

With that in mind, I really wasn't thinking about writing a book about slow-cooker cooking (does anyone?). Our oldest daughter, Maren, had asked me to write out some of her favorite dishes, like Moroccan Lamb Stew, so she would have some-thing to cook when she graduates college and gets her first apartment. After writing out about ten recipes, I realized I had a lot of them and I could easily put them into a book. So, here we are, slow-cooker in hand and ready to go. I have included a recipe for every week of the year, so you can be a dinner superhero too. These are all recipes I have made and my own family enjoyed. If you like seafood, sorry, I am not a seafood fan. I rank seafood right up there with the *Hotdogger* (and you know what that tastes like). So, nothing that breathes water is in this book (though I realize that is not something to be overly proud of). Regardless, I think you will enjoy trying the different recipes. Some you will make exactly as written, others you will try your own twists and turns. But, if you like to eat and want to create amazing flavors and smells, I am very confident you will use this book a lot – say, at least once a week. And always remember – low and slow is the way to go!

Dedication

would like to dedicate this book to my lovely and talented wife, Inger, who is the *real* cook in the family. And to our amazing daughters, Maren and Zoey, who encouraged me to keep cooking with the slow-cooker and who always give me their honest (and sometimes brutal) opinion of how it turned out. But most of all to my mom and dad, Carole and Tom Miller, who always fed me!

A (Very) Brief History of Slow Cooking

I wish I could have been there when our cavemen ancestors realized the wonderfulness of slow-cooking. Someway, somehow, shortly after the discovery of fire for cooking, Neanderthal Ned discovered that letting his mammoth ribs cook slowly over the fire greatly enhanced the flavor and tenderness of the meat. Pretty awesome. Yet, most of us do not have an open pit fire to slowly cook our food (or the time to stand outside and tend the fire and the food). So, let's fast forward to the Romans. I know it seems like a whole lot of stuff gets attributed to the Romans (same for the Greeks and Chinese) but we do have to recognize their contribution to slow-cooking – the cooking pot. Sure, they may have stolen the idea from some people they killed, but they perfected the use of a clay jar to slowly braise meat and vegetables, to make what we today call a stew. And for that reason alone, I am willing to overlook a lot of things. So, let's not quibble if a few Goths and Visigoths got clubbed to death or run-through with a gladius short-sword, it all worked out fine in the end.

For our purposes, and skipping over a lot of centuries of slow cooking, that end was 1940 when Irving Nachumsohn received a patent for the device that ultimately became the Crock-Pot®. He invented it as a way to cook cholent, a traditional Jewish stew made with potatoes, beef, and beans. His grandmother made this dish by leaving a ceramic crock full of the ingredients near the large ovens of their bakery, where the indirect heat would cook the stew slowly overnight, so it would be ready on the Jewish Sabbath (a day when cooking is prohibited). His innovation over grandma's bakery scam was to place the crockery into an encased heating element so that electricity would take the place of the bakery ovens – and modern day "low and slow" was invented!

For decades, the device was known as the "Beanery" which I can see now may have impacted sales unless you really love beans and want a device apparently devoted to cooking them. The slow-cooker really took off in the 1970's when Rival bought the Beanery and changed its name to the "Crock Pot" or the *Original Slow Electric Stoneware Cooker* (yea, Crock Pot is way better). One reason for its popularity at this time (and not just the name change) was the wave of women entering the work force in the USA. While now seen as sadly sexist, the Crock Pot was marketed as a way for women to have dinner ready when they got home (vs. having to start cooking after work). Apparently, men weren't into cooking dinner back the 1970's (which now that I reflect back on that time is actually pretty true). But, hopefully, this book will help change that! Another reason slow-cookers surged in popularity in the 1970's was high inflation along with the first gas crisis. A slow cooker uses about the same amount of electricity as a light bulb making it very economical when things get tight financially, and it makes cheaper cuts of meat taste wonderful. Additionally, in 1975, Mable Hoffman released her *Crockery Cookery* book which duked it out with *The Joy of Sex* for bestseller of 1975. Unfortunate title aside, this book revealed the versatility of the slow-cooker and helped boost sales for the rest of the decade. Sadly, the Crock-Pot's popularity did not last. The microwave oven came on the scene in the 1980's and quickly became the appliance of choice for getting dinner ready when time was short (and don't forget the *Hotdogger* was now in many American homes too, ready to electrocute as many hotdogs as necessary to get dinner on the table).

Like many things, what's old becomes new again and the slow-cooker has made a revival over the past decade. This is due not only to the rediscovery of the wonderfulness of slow-cooking, but also to a change in how slow-cooker meals are prepared. Long gone are the days of "dump and go" and if that's your plan this book is not for you. Taking time and care with preparation, using fresh ingredients, and experimenting with herbs and spices have led to a new interest in the slow-cooker as a way to cook - and not just save time. Because the only limit is your imagination, get ready to take your place in the next generation of slow-cooker greats. Oh, and if you want to talk about the Instant-Pot® as a substitute for the slow-cooker because it cooks "faster," you need to … um, buy a different book (not what I originally wrote that you should do, but the editor started hyperventilating).

What Gear Will I Need?

The good news is that you do not need a lot of stuff to get started with slow cooking. Here are the basic tools (many of which you probably already own):

- Six-quart slow-cooker
- Set of measuring spoons
- Set of measuring cups (for solids)
- Two-cup glass measuring cup (for liquids)
- Large cutting board
- Paring knife
- Chef's knife
- Wooden spoon (use wooden spoon vs. plastic)
- Spatula set
- Can opener
- Metal whisk
- Box grater
- Blender (or food processor)
- Vegetable peeler
- Tongs
- Frying pan
- Set of mixing bowls
- Chopper tool (e.g., a Ninja, ™ or string pull)

- YouTube – if you're not sure how to do something, look for a video on YouTube (or call your mom)!
- Amazon – can't find the right spice or kitchen tool? Odds are good you can get it on Amazon

Ten Things You Need to Know About Using a Slow-Cooker

(Read This Before You Start!)

There are a few things I have learned about using a slow-cooker and I want to share those with you here. If you take these to heart, your slow cooking adventures will turn out well, and often times fantastic.

1. **Brown the meat and onions before you put it into the slow-cooker.** There are only a few recipes in the book that do not tell you to brown the meat. Browning the meat creates an incredible depth of flavor and gives you a great color (which is important to making a meal appetizing). Do not skip this step! If you dredge meat in flour before browning, you will get a thicker sauce. And always brown ground beef! For almost any recipe that calls for onions, you should brown the onions first. You will enjoy the flavor imparted by the slight caramelization of the onions as the sugars break down.

2. **Read the recipe.** Before you start cutting, chopping, browning, or whatever, stop and read the entire recipe. For example, some of these recipes require that you marinade the meat overnight. You'll want to know that before you start. And, if you are having guests and want to impress them with your slow-cooker skills, don't let that be the first time you try the recipe. Make it one

time without any pressure, e.g., just your hungry *regular* family. That way, if it fails, all the mocking comes from a place of love – I think (wow, really starting to flash back here as I write this).

3. **Let it sit overnight if you can/freeze it**. Turn off the slow-cooker a little early and let it cool a bit, then place in the refrigerator overnight. The flavors will deepen tremendously. The added benefit is that you can scoop off some of the fat that will congeal on the surface. Also, most slow-cooker soups, stews, and sauces freeze well. So, don't worry about big portions. Most of the recipes in this book easily serve around 6-8 people.

4. **Don't use the "high" setting**. It may be tempting to save a little time but don't. Always use the "low" setting and let your meal cook low and slow. The high setting can also toughen meats, which is the exact opposite of what you hope to (and will) achieve with the low setting. That said, if a recipe (e.g., risotto) calls for a high setting, use it.

5. **Trim the fat**. Some fat is fine (it adds flavor), but you will be much happier with your meal if you trim a good bit of the fat off of the meat you are cooking.

6. **Get a least a 6-quart slow-cooker**. There are many sizes of slow-cookers but the most versatile is the 6-quart size. It's big enough for most families, but small enough that you can cut recipes down if you need to. If you have a big dinner you're cooking for, just buy a second slow-cooker. It's a relatively inexpensive way to give yourself flexibility. Your slow-cooker should not be filled to the brim when you cook. Two-thirds full is ideal.

7. **Use broth instead of water**. If your recipe calls for adding water (rare), use chicken or beef stock or broth as a substitute. It will add flavor and depth. In a pinch, however, and if liquid is needed, you can certainly add a little water. But, the great thing about the slow-cooker is that most of moisture you will need is already contained in the ingredients, and the braising in the slow-cooker will draw all that moisture out. So, don't add liquid unless the recipe says to. And if you find yourself with too much liquid in the slow-cooker you can thicken things up by removing the lid (or moving it off center) and letting the moisture evaporate for 30-45 minutes.

8. **Salt and pepper**. Two pretty basic ingredients for most recipes. Use coarse/ sea salt and fresh ground pepper if you can. Flavors are much better! You can certainly use regular salt and pre-ground pepper. And, once you get started,

it's probably time to update the spices in your pantry. That oregano from the Bill Clinton administration is not going to do what you need it to do.

9. **Precision is not required**. For each recipe in this book, you will see measurements for ingredients. While it's important to come close to those measurements, you don't need to be fanatical about measuring *exactly* ¼ teaspoon or *exactly* two pounds of stew meat. Close enough counts with a slow-cooker. That said, I always like to go a little over vs. a little under.

10. **Experiment**! Recipes are great, but, like the Pirates' Code, you should view them as more of a guideline. There is always room to experiment, especially with a slow-cooker because it is so forgiving. Basically, unless you leave it on too long and your meal dries out, or you mess up tablespoon and teaspoon, it is very difficult to ruin something with a slow-cooker. Just about every recipe in this book is a version of another recipe. I tried different things with each to come up with a version that my family likes. You might like everything exactly as I have laid it out or you might want to use more pepper or oregano, substitute chicken breasts for thighs, add carrots or celery to everything, or never use onions. That's fine. It is completely up to you and your tastes and the tastes of your family. I suggest that you try each recipe pretty close to how I have laid it out and see what you like or don't like about it. Then next time you make it, you can change it up. Trust me, I did that a lot. You can also make changes while it's cooking. You can add spices and herbs at any time during the cooking process – though you should let it cook several hours before deciding whether anything more is needed.

So, that's it for my tips. Time to get cooking! The recipes are in no particular order (despite editor requests otherwise) so just skip around and find things you might like to try. Oh, and the photos are just for show because I know that people like to look at a photo when cooking. I just bought these from a service because I am *way* too lazy to sit around and take pictures of stuff I cook. I just eat it.

Finally, if this is your first-time cooking with a slow-cooker, I recommend you try the pot roast or beef stew first (those are the first two recipes). And always take your time and enjoy the cooking journey. You will certainly enjoy the results!

Sterling Miller

August 2018

Pot Roast

"The American classic! Perfect any time of year."

Ingredients

3 lbs. boneless Chuck roast

1 medium yellow onion (chopped)

2 14.5 oz. cans beef broth/stock

8 – 16 oz. fresh sliced Cremini (or Portabella) mushrooms

2-3 stalks of celery (chopped)

15- 20 baby carrots

7-10 small yellow or red potatoes (skins on/quartered)

3 large cloves garlic (minced)

Sea salt/coarse salt

Ground black pepper

1 tablespoon olive oil

2-3 tablespoons butter

Instructions

Spray slow-cooker with non-stick cooking spray. Turn to low.

Pour olive oil into frying pan. Rub roast with salt and pepper to taste. Brown roast on both sides on medium heat. Place in slow-cooker along with one can of beef both/stock (use second can as needed during cooking process).

Add mushrooms, celery, potatoes, and carrots to slow-cooker on top of roast. Cover.

Drain any grease from frying pan (but do not clean). Add 2-3 tablespoons of butter. On medium heat, brown onions in pan - stirring frequently. When you think you have about a minute left to brown onions, stir in the garlic. Cook for a minute then add onions and garlic to slow-cooker.

Cook on low for 8 hours (or until desired tenderness). Skim visible fat.

Notes

Have fun and experiment as it is almost impossible to mess this up. Add or subtract vegetables as you see fit. Canned corn or zucchini make great additions. Experiment with other spices, such as rosemary, thyme or tarragon.

Beef Stew

"Nothing says 'love' like a bowl of this!"

Ingredients

2-3 lbs. beef stew meat (or cut up Chuck roast into 1-inch cubes)

1 medium yellow onion (chopped)

2 14.5 oz. cans beef broth/stock (can also mix half/half with chicken broth/stock)

8 – 16 oz. fresh sliced Cremini (or Portabella) mushrooms

1 14.5 oz. can of sweet corn (optional)

2-3 stalks of celery (chopped)

24 baby carrots (or two big handfuls). You can also use 4 large carrots, peeled and sliced

7-10 small yellow or red potatoes (skins on/quartered). You can also cut up regular size potatoes

3 large cloves garlic (minced)

2 bay leaves (optional)

1 teaspoon sea salt/coarse salt

½ teaspoon ground black pepper

3 tablespoons flour

1 tablespoon olive oil

2-3 tablespoons butter

Instructions

Spray slow-cooker with non-stick cooking spray. Turn to low.

Pour olive oil into frying pan. Place stew meat in large plastic bag with flour, salt and pepper. Shake to coat and then brown meat on medium heat (may have to brown in batches). Place in slow-cooker along with beef both/stock (more broth/stock may be needed during cooking process).

Add mushrooms, celery, potatoes, corn, and carrots to slow-cooker. Cover.

Drain any grease from frying pan (but do not clean). Add 2-3 tablespoons of butter. On medium heat, brown onions in pan - stirring frequently. When you think you have about a minute left to brown onions, stir in the garlic. Cook for a minute then add onions and garlic to slow-cooker.

Cook on low for 8 hours (or until desired tenderness). Skim visible fat.

Notes

Cooked/crumbled bacon can be a nice addition. Add or subtract vegetables as you see fit. Experiment with other spices, such as rosemary, thyme or tarragon. Adding a ¼ cup of Worcester sauce can be good as well. Serve with crusty bread.

Green Chile Posole

"The recipe that started it all for me!"

Ingredients

2-3 lbs. of boneless pork ribs, trimmed of most fat, and cut into 1-inch cubes (you can also use pork loin or boneless pork chops)

1 medium yellow onion (chopped)

3 15 oz. cans of white hominy (you can go with more or less depending on your taste)

1 4 oz. can diced green chiles (mild, medium, or hot to suit your taste)

5 large cloves of garlic (minced)

½ to 1 teaspoon of cayenne pepper (to taste)

2 teaspoons dried Mexican oregano

½ teaspoon salt (coarse is better)

2 14.5 oz. cans chicken broth/stock

1 tablespoon olive oil

2-3 tablespoons butter

Instructions

Spray slow-cooker with non-stick cooking spray. Turn to low.

Pour olive oil into frying pan. Brown pork on medium heat. Place in slow-cooker along with chicken broth.

Add green chiles, cayenne pepper, Mexican oregano, salt, and hominy.

Drain any grease from frying pan (but do not clean). Add 2-3 tablespoons of butter. On medium heat, brown onions in pan - stirring frequently. When you think you have about a minute left to brown onions, stir in the garlic. Cook for a minute then add onions and garlic to slow-cooker.

Cook on low for 6-8 hours (or until pork is at desired tenderness). You may need to add additional broth the longer you cook it.

Notes

Serve with corn bread or warm corn/flour tortillas. You can also add shredded Monterey Jack cheese when serving.

Rojo (Red) Posole

"Green Posole's red-hot sister!"

Ingredients

2 - 3 lbs. of boneless pork ribs, trimmed of fat, and cut into 1-inch cubes (you can also use pork shoulder or pork stew meat)

1 medium yellow onion (diced)

5 large cloves garlic (minced)

2 14.5 oz. cans of chicken broth/stock

1 28 oz. can of red enchilada sauce

2 4 oz. cans of diced green chiles (hot, medium, or mild to suit your taste)

2 chipotle chiles in adobo sauce (you will have to buy a small can most likely)

2 28 oz. cans of white hominy (rinse and drain)

Coarse salt

Black pepper

2 teaspoons ground cumin

¼ teaspoon Mexican oregano (crush between your fingers)

2 teaspoons olive oil

Optional (for garnish): sliced radish, shredded cabbage, cilantro (chopped), shredded Monterey Jack cheese, queso fresco cheese, lime wedges, avocado slices

Instructions

Spray slow-cooker with non-stick cooking spray. Turn to low.

Pour olive oil into frying pan. Season pork with salt and pepper to taste and then brown pork on medium heat. Cook in batches if needed. Place in slow-cooker along with chicken broth and enchilada sauce.

Add green chiles, cumin, Mexican oregano, chipotle chiles, and hominy.

Drain any grease from frying pan (but do not clean). Add 2-3 tablespoons of butter. On medium heat, brown onions in pan - stirring frequently. When you think you have about a minute left to brown onions, stir in the garlic. Cook for a minute then add onions and garlic to slow-cooker.

Cook on low for 8 hours (or until pork is at desired tenderness). You may need to add additional broth the longer you cook it.

Notes

Serve with corn bread or warm corn/flour tortillas. Add garnishes to taste.

Marrakesh Lamb Stew

"Made Zoey love lamb all over again!"

Ingredients

2 ½-3 lbs. leg of lamb (boneless, trim fat, cut into 1-inch cubes)

1 medium yellow onion (chopped)

5 large cloves garlic (minced)

1 14.5 oz. can of diced tomatoes (do not drain)

1 14.5 oz. can(s) of chickpeas (drained/rinsed)

12 dried apricots (cut in halves)

¼ cup raisins

1 14.5 oz. can of chicken broth/stock

1 tablespoon fresh ginger root (minced)

1 tablespoon cumin

½ teaspoon cayenne pepper

¼ teaspoon cinnamon

2 teaspoons coriander

Coarse salt

Black pepper

2 teaspoons olive oil

2-3 tablespoons of butter

Instructions

Spray slow-cooker with non-stick cooking spray. Turn to low.

Pour olive oil into frying pan. Season lamb with salt and pepper to taste and then brown on medium heat. You may need to cook in batches. Place in slow-cooker.

Drain any grease from frying pan (but do not clean). Add 2-3 tablespoons of butter. Brown onions in pan - stirring frequently. When browned, add garlic, ginger, cumin, cinnamon, and cayenne pepper. Cook for two minutes on medium heat. Add broth/stock and diced tomatoes. Bring to a boil.

Add mixture to slow-cooker along with raisins and apricots.

Cook on low for 6-7 hours (or until lamb is at desired tenderness).

Notes

You can delete either the raisins or the apricots, but not both. Serve on white rice, egg noodles, or couscous. A spoon of Greek yogurt or Tzatziki sauce is nice garnish. Warm naan flat bread with butter goes great with this dish.

Hungarian Goulash

"Went to Budapest, now I love goulash!"

Ingredients

3 lbs. beef chuck roast (or stew meat or boneless short-ribs)

2 14.5 oz. cans beef broth/stock (chicken broth/stock works too)

4 tablespoons tomato paste

2 tablespoons Worcestershire sauce

¼ cup Hungarian paprika (*use Hungarian*!)

¼ cup brown sugar

3 teaspoons dry mustard powder

5 medium potatoes (red or yellow) cubed or wedged

1 medium or large yellow onion (chopped)

12 – 16 oz. fresh sliced Cremini (or Portabella) mushrooms

20 baby carrots (more or less to taste)

4 large cloves garlic (minced)

1 teaspoon cumin

Coarse salt

Black pepper

2 tablespoons olive oil

2-3 tablespoons butter

¼ cup flour

Instructions

Spray slow-cooker with non-stick cooking spray. Turn to low.

Pour olive oil into frying pan. Season beef with salt and pepper to taste and then brown on medium heat. You may need to cook in batches. Place in slow-cooker along with beef broth.

In bowl, mix together tomato paste, Worcestershire sauce, paprika, brown sugar, mustard powder, and cumin. Add to slow-cooker along with potatoes, mushrooms, and carrots.

Drain any grease from frying pan (but do not clean). Add 2-3 tablespoons of butter. Brown onions in pan - stirring frequently. When you think you have about a minute left to brown onions, stir in the garlic. Cook for a minute then add onions and garlic to slow-cooker. Cover and cook on low for 8-10 hours. About 20 minutes before you plan on serving, dissolve flour in small amount of water and add to cooker. Turn to high and allow goulash to slightly thicken.

Notes

Serve with egg noodles and with crusty bread. Garnish with sour cream and chopped parsley.

Rack of Lamb

"Rack of lamb in a slow-cooker? Hell yes!"

Ingredients

1 to 2 racks of lamb (about 2-4 lbs.). Trim most (not all) fat (and yes, lamb does smell a bit funky so don't worry). Slice between ribs into serving size pieces, e.g., two "ribs" per serving"

3 tablespoons olive oil

Coarse salt

Black pepper

1 medium – large yellow onion (chopped roughly)

2-3 stalks of celery (chopped roughly)

8 – 16 oz. fresh sliced Cremini (or Portabella) mushrooms

10-20 baby carrots (or 3 carrots chopped)

6-8 small red potatoes, skin-on, cut into quarters

6 large cloves of garlic (smashed)

1½ cups red wine

1 tablespoon rosemary

1 tablespoon thyme

3 bay leaves

2-3 tablespoons of butter

Instructions

Spray slow-cooker with non-stick cooking spray. Turn to low.

Pour olive oil into frying pan. Season lamb with salt and pepper to taste and then brown on all sides on medium heat. You will need to cook in batches. Place in slow-cooker.

Drain any grease from frying pan (but do not clean). Add 2-3 tablespoons of butter. Brown onions in pan on medium heat - stirring frequently. When you think you have about a minute left to brown onions, add the smashed garlic. Cook for a minute then add onions and garlic to slow-cooker.

Add wine, celery, carrots, mushroom, potatoes to slow cooker.

Sprinkle rosemary and thyme evenly over contents of slow-cooker. Add bay leaves. Cover and cook on low for 8-10 hours.

Notes

Use sauce in slow-cooker on lamb. Garnish with feta cheese. Serve with side salad, crusty bread and/or couscous. Experiment and try other spices you like, e.g., Herbs de Provence, fresh rosemary, etc.

Pork Carnitas

"Make it once, use it for five different meals!"

Ingredients

4 lbs. boneless pork shoulder/butt (*do not* use pork loin – too lean). Trim most fat but leave nice amount for flavor

2-3 jalapeno peppers (seeded/ribs removed). Chopped coarsely. Or use 4 oz. can diced green chilies (hot or medium). You can also use both if you wish

6 large cloves garlic (minced)

2 oranges (for juice only)

2 limes (for juice only)

1 medium/large yellow onion

2 tablespoons coarse salt

2 teaspoons black pepper

1 ½ tablespoons chili powder

2 teaspoons ground cumin

2 ½ teaspoons Mexican oregano

2 tablespoons olive oil

2-3 tablespoons butter

Instructions

Spray slow-cooker with non-stick cooking spray. Turn to low.

Create a rub by combining salt, pepper, chili powder, Mexican oregano, cumin, and olive oil in small bowl.

Rinse and dry pork shoulder then season with rub mixture above, rubbing thoroughly on all sides. Place in slow-cooker.

Place 2-3 tablespoons of butter in frying pan. Brown onions in pan on medium heat - stirring frequently. When you think you have about a minute left to brown onions, add the minced garlic. Cook for a minute then add onions and garlic to slow-cooker.

Add jalapenos/green chilies and juice from oranges and limes to slow-cooker. Cover on cook on low for 8-10 hours (or until meat is very tender). Remove meat from slow-cooker and shred using forks. Return to slow-cooker for 30 more minutes on warm.

Preheat oven to "broil." When ready, place meat on large baking sheet and broil until crisp (about 3-5 minutes). Get a nice brown crust on meat. Remove from oven and serve.

Ham and Bean Soup

"So easy, so good!"

Ingredients

1 20 oz. package of "15 bean" soup mix (you can find this in the pasta/dry bean section at your grocery store)

1 ham steak (cubed). Approximately 1 ½ lbs. Keep the bone. You can also use several ham hocks or pre-cooked/smoked sausage. Cooked chicken works great too

1 ½ teaspoons chili powder

8 cups (64 oz.) of chicken broth or stock

3 bay leaves

Optional: 1 medium chopped yellow onion (sauté')

Instructions

Soak beans in water over night.

Spray slow-cooker with non-stick cooking spray. Turn to low.

Add beans (drained and rinsed), chicken broth/stock, chili powder, bay leaves, and meat. You can brown the pre-cooked sausage if you want. Slice sausage up before adding to slow-cooker.

Cover and cook on low 6-8 hours (you may need to add additional chicken broth/stock).

Notes

Serve with cornbread or crusty bread. You can also garnish with shredded parmesan cheese.

Mom's Mac & Cheese

"Maren's favorite food group – cheesy pasta!"

Ingredients

1 pint of whole milk (do not use skim or low-fat milk. You can use Half & Half if you want)

1 lb. box of Kraft Velveeta cheese (cut up in cubes)

1 lb. package of elbow macaroni (or your preferred pasta, e.g., shells, rotini, etc.)

Coarse salt

Black pepper

1 tablespoon flour

6 table spoons butter

Optional: cubed ham steak

Instructions

Boil water in large pot. Add salt. When water is boiling, add macaroni. Cook to *al dente* (read package for cooking instructions). Rinse macaroni in hot water and set aside.

In large glass or ceramic bowl (don't use plastic) place butter and melt in microwave – watch closely as it will melt fast. Remove bowl and add 1 tablespoon of flour to the melted butter. Whisk until smooth.

Add 1 cup of milk. Whisk. If not smooth add small amounts of milk until smooth. Add Velveeta and place back in microwave. Heat in short bursts, i.e., 30 seconds and take out and stir until you get a smooth, creamy cheese sauce.

Turn on slow-cooker to low, spray with non-stick cooking spray and grease lightly with some butter.

Add macaroni and salt and pepper to taste – mix well. Mix in cheese sauce and, if you want, ham.

Cover and cook on low for two hours.

Notes

This makes a great side dish or a meal in itself.

Five Star Sloppy Joes

"Perfect for poker night!"

Ingredients

1 ½ lbs. ground beef (80/20)

1 lbs. packaged ground pork

1 small/medium yellow onion (diced)

3 large cloves garlic (minced)

½ teaspoon salt

½ teaspoon black pepper

½ teaspoon garlic powder

2-3 tablespoons Worcestershire sauce

2 tablespoons yellow mustard

¼ cup brown sugar (firmly packed)

¼ cup flour

1 cup ketchup

¾ cup BBQ sauce (spicy or flavor to taste)

1 tablespoon chili powder

Optional: ½ green bell pepper

1 package hamburger buns (or gourmet buns or rolls, i.e., poppy seed, pretzel, ciabatta, French)

3 tablespoons butter

Instructions

Turn on slow-cooker to low, spray with non-stick cooking spray.

Place 2-3 tablespoons of butter in frying pan. Brown onions in pan on medium heat - stirring frequently. Add ground beef and pork and brown until crumbly and no longer pink. When you think you have about a minute left, add the minced garlic. Cook for another minute then drain fat from mixture by placing on large plate covered with a paper towel. Add to slow-cooker.

Add salt, pepper, garlic powder, Worcestershire sauce, yellow mustard, brown sugar, ketchup, BBQ sauce, chili powder to a large bowl and mix together. Pour the sauce over the ground beef and pork mixture in the slow-cooker. Add flour and stir everything together.

Cover and cook on low for 5 hours.

Serve on buns (toasted buns are better!)

Notes

Adjust spices/ingredients to taste. For extra kick, you can add jalapeno or green chilies.

Dixie Roast

"Waiting for you on Sunday, right after church!"

Ingredients

1 3-4 lbs. boneless Chuck roast. You can also use brisket or Bottom Round roast

1 stick of butter

1 package Ranch dry mix

1 package Au Jus gravy mix

¼ cup beef broth

2-3 teaspoons coarse salt

2-3 teaspoons black pepper

¼ cup flour

10-12 pepperoncini peppers (these are very mild so don't worry about "heat")

3-4 tablespoons vegetable or canola oil (olive oil is fine as well)

Optional: Dry onion soup mix and/or 10 baby red or white potatoes sliced in half (skins on)

Instructions

Turn on slow-cooker to low, spray with non-stick cooking spray.

Combine salt, pepper, and flour and then rub on roast – work into all areas of the meat.

Using high heat, add oil to frying pan and then sear roast on both sides (5 minutes per side – try to create a crust). Remove from pan and place in slow-cooker.

Sprinkle ranch dressing and au jus mixes over roast. If using dry onion mix, add as well.

Place butter and pepperoncini on top of roast. If adding potatoes, place around the roast. Add ¼ cup beef broth. Cover and cook on low 6-8 hours.

Notes

Garnish with chopped parsley. Serve with egg noodles or mash potatoes (if you don't add potatoes). This also makes great sandwiches on hard rolls.

Chicken Risotto

"Amazing flavors, perfectly combined!"

Ingredients

1 ¾ cups Arborio rice (must be Arborio, *do not* use regular rice)

8 oz. Portabella or Cremini mushrooms (sliced)

¼ to ½ small yellow onion (finely diced) or 1 shallot (finely diced)

1 large garlic clove (minced)

2 large chicken breasts (cooked and shredded). You can also use store-bought rotisserie chicken

4 cups chicken broth/stock

1 teaspoon salt

1 teaspoon black pepper

1-2 tablespoons lemon juice

½ cup Parmesan cheese (shredded)

6 tablespoons butter

Instructions

Turn on slow-cooker to low, spray with non-stick cooking spray.

Place 4 tablespoons of butter in large frying pan. Brown mushrooms, shallot/onions, and garlic in pan on medium heat - stirring frequently. About 5-6 minutes. Add Arborio rice and stir for about 2-3 minutes until well coated. Add to slow-cooker.

Add chicken broth, salt, pepper, and shredded chicken to rice mixture in slow-cooker. Stir.

Cover and cook on high for 1 ½ to 2 hours. Check it at 1 ½ hour mark (or a little sooner). Rice must be tender and liquid absorbed.

Once cooked, stir in additional butter and more salt and pepper to taste. Add parmesan cheese. Mix well.

Notes

You can add 1 cup cooked peas at the end if you want. Serve with crusty bread. This is a recipe you might have to play with a bit to get texture and flavors right for your family.

Barley and Beef Soup

"So good you'll want to eat it every day!"

Ingredients

2 ½-3 lbs. stew meat, trimmed of excess fat. Cut into small pieces

1 large yellow onion (finely chopped)

8 - 12 oz. Portabella mushrooms (chopped)

5 large cloves garlic (minced)

12 cups beef broth/stock

1 cup pearl barley

¼ cup tomato paste

4 stalks celery (chopped)

2-3 carrots (chopped very fine)

½ cup fresh parsley (divided)

1 teaspoon dried thyme

Coarse salt

Black pepper

1 jalapeno pepper (diced)

½ cup red wine

2-3 tablespoons butter

3 tablespoons olive oil

Instructions

Turn on slow-cooker to low, spray with non-stick cooking spray.

Heat olive oil in large frying pan – high/medium heat. Generously season stew meat with salt and pepper. Brown in pan (you may have to cook in batches). Transfer meat and juices to slow-cooker.

Add broth, carrots, celery, tomato paste, wine, barley, ¼ cup of parsley, thyme, jalapeno, and mushrooms to slow-cooker.

Place 2-3 tablespoons of butter in frying pan on medium heat. Brown onions in pan - stirring frequently. When you think you have about a minute left to brown onions, add the minced garlic. Cook for a minute then add onions and garlic to slow-cooker.

Cover and cook on low for 6-8 hours – until meat is very tender. Garnish with remaining parsley to taste.

Notes:

Serve with crusty bread. You can also garnish with shredded parmesan cheese. The barley will soak up a lot of liquid, so you may need to add more broth/stock.

Chicken Tortilla Soup

"A New Mexican favorite that's even better the second day!"

Ingredients

2 -2½ lbs. of chicken (mix of skinless and boneless breasts and skinless/boneless thighs)

1 15 oz. can of crushed tomatoes

1 15 oz. can black beans (drained and rinsed)

1 15 oz. can corn (add a second can if you really like corn)

1 10 oz. can red enchilada sauce

1 medium yellow onion (coarsely chopped)

3 jalapeno peppers (seeded and chopped)

1 4 oz. can diced green chiles (hot, medium, mild to taste). Or, fresh green chiles if in season

4 cups chicken broth/stock

1 lime

4-5 large cloves garlic (smashed)

1 teaspoon cumin

1 -2 tablespoons fresh cilantro (chopped)

1 ½ teaspoons chili powder

1 teaspoon black pepper

Shredded Monterey Jack cheese

1 small bag tortilla chips

Instructions

Turn on slow-cooker to low, spray with non-stick cooking spray.

Place raw chicken on bottom of slow cooker.

In blender (or food processor) combine crushed tomatoes, enchilada sauce, onions, jalapenos, garlic, and 1 cup of chicken broth (or less if blender full). Blend until smooth.

Pour mixture over chicken and add green chiles, cumin, chili powder, corn, black pepper, rest of chicken broth/stock, and juice of one lime. Mix together well then add cilantro.

Cover and cook on low for 8 hours. At about 7 hours, remove chicken and shred with fork. Return chicken to slow-cooker. Serve with tortilla chips and Monterey Jack cheese in soup.

Notes

Fresh avocados chunks, sour cream, and additional lime wedges are nice additions when serving.

Pollo de "Monica"

"Thank you, Monica, for giving me this Swiss Army Knife of chicken!"

Ingredients

2 lbs. boneless chicken breasts (you can also use boneless chicken thighs, or mix breast and thigh meat)

1 cup chicken broth/stock

¼ cup Knorr™ Caldo Con Sabor de Pollo chicken flavored bouillon mix (you'll find this in the soup or Mexican food sections at grocery store)

1 4 oz. can diced green chiles (hot, medium, mild to taste)

Instructions

Turn on slow-cooker to low, spray with non-stick cooking spray.

Place raw chicken on bottom of slow cooker.

In bowl, mix brock/stock and bouillon. Pour over chicken.

Add green chiles. Cover and cook on low for 6-8 hours.

At 5-hour mark, take chicken from slow-cooker and shred meat with fork. Return to slow-cooker and let cook until meat is very tender.

If too "soupy" you can move cover so some heat escapes and let mixture cook down some.

Notes

This is a very versatile meal. You can eat this as the main course or you can use this as filler for tacos or tostados. It can also be used for taco salad, burritos, and enchiladas. You can add a can of corn (drained) to the mixture as an option. Serve with guacamole and tortillas. A side of Spanish rice completes the meal.

French Cassoulet

"You won't believe how good this is!"

Ingredients

1 lbs. boneless pork shoulder (cut into 1-inch pieces)

1 lbs. boneless chicken breasts or boneless chicken thighs (or mixture of both)

1 lbs. smoked chorizo sausages or other fully cooked sausage if chorizo not available (you can also cook any type of sausage and use that)

5-6 thick cut slices of bacon

1 lbs. bag of white beans (e.g., navy)

5 large cloves of garlic (crushed)

1 teaspoon dried thyme

1 15 oz. can chopped/diced plum tomatoes

1 medium/large yellow onion (chopped)

1 bay leaf

1 ½ cups of bread crumbs or panko tossed in 2 tablespoons olive oil

4 cups chicken broth/stock

2 bay leaves

2-3 tablespoons of olive oil

3-4 tablespoons butter

Coarse salt and black pepper

Instructions

Rinse and soak beans overnight.

Turn on slow-cooker to low, spray with non-stick cooking spray. Add beans (drained and rinsed).

Heat olive oil in large frying pan – medium heat. Brown chicken on both sides then place on bottom of slow cooker. Season pork with salt and pepper. Brown in pan then transfer meat and juices to slow-cooker. Cook bacon in same pan. Let drain on paper towel then crumble/add to slow-cooker.

Place 2-3 tablespoons of butter in frying pan on medium heat. Brown onions in pan - stirring frequently. When you think you have about a minute left to brown onions, add the crushed garlic. Cook for a minute then add onions and garlic to slow-cooker mixture.

Add thyme, tomatoes (with juice), bay leaf, and chicken broth/stock. You want to use enough chicken broth or stock to cover mixture by about 2 inches.

Cover and cook on low for 8 hours, until meat is very tender, and beans are soft. Just prior to serving, toast bread crumb mixture in a skillet on medium heat and then sprinkle mixture over the cassoulet.

Notes

Experiment with different meats and spices. Cassoulet means "whatever is lying around," so raid the leftovers, the pantry and the freezer to create your own family favorite.

Chicken Cacciatore

"Spectacular chicken and sauce meal!"

Ingredients

4-6 boneless chicken breast halves (you can also use chicken thighs)

1 6 oz. can of tomato paste

8 - 12 oz. Portabella or Cremini mushrooms

1 small yellow onion (finely chopped)

8-10 cloves of garlic (minced)

2 teaspoons dried oregano

1 teaspoon dried basil

1 teaspoon black pepper

½ teaspoon red pepper flakes

½ to a whole green pepper (seeded and coarsely chopped)

1 28 oz. jar of pre-made marinara sauce

Optional: ½ cup red wine

1 box of thin spaghetti or angel hair pasta (but any pasta will do in a pinch)

2-3 tablespoons of olive oil

2-3 tablespoons of butter

Grated or shredded parmesan or romano (sharp) cheese

Instructions

Turn on slow-cooker to low, spray with non-stick cooking spray.

Heat olive oil in large frying pan – medium heat. Brown chicken on both sides then place on bottom of slow cooker. Add marinara sauce and red wine.

Place 2-3 tablespoons of butter in frying pan on medium heat. Brown onions in pan - stirring frequently. When you think you have about a minute left to brown onions, add the minced garlic. Cook for a minute then add onions and garlic to slow-cooker mixture.

Add tomato paste, oregano, basil, mushrooms, pepper, green pepper, and red pepper flakes. Cover and cook on low for 6-8 hours until chicken is tender.

Cook pasta per instructions on box.

Serve cacciatore over the pasta and garnish with parmesan or romano cheese to taste.

Notes

Serve with garlic bread. You can make the green pepper and red pepper flakes optional. You can also reduce or increase minced garlic. Depends on taste. Keep an extra jar of marinara sauce handy.

Aloha Pork Roast

"It's like being at a luau on the beach in Maui!"

Ingredients

6 lbs. pork shoulder/butt roast

2 bananas (sliced open/left in peel)

1 ½ tablespoons red Hawaiian sea salt (can order on-line or specialty grocer). If you use other salt you will likely need less as Hawaiian sea salt is not as salty

1 tablespoon liquid smoke

1 cup chicken broth/stock

Optional: 1 habanero pepper (use 4-5 small slices)

White rice

Hawaiian sweet rolls/buns

Instructions

Turn on slow-cooker to low, spray with non-stick cooking spray.

Pierce pork roast all over with fork.

Rub salt all over pork roast, into crevices, etc. Next, rub liquid smoke over pork roast (use gloves/baggies to protect hands as smoke smell is hard to wash off).

Place roast in slow-cooker. Add broth/stock and habanero (if used). Place bananas on top of roast.

Cover and cook for 16-20 hours on low under meat is very tender. Turn roast halfway through cooking time. With about an hour to go, remove meat and shred it with fork. Return to slow-cooker for one more hour to soak in juices. Remove banana peels.

Serve on buns with rice, or on top of bed of rice.

Notes

This dish is meant to be salty, but you can adjust salt to your taste. If worried, start with less and then add more later in cooking process. If you don't use red Hawaiian sea salt, you will probably need a tablespoon of salt. When serving you can also use BBQ sauce and coleslaw is good to serve with this pork dish as well.

Lonestar BBQ Brisket

"Everything's bigger in Texas, especially flavor!"

Ingredients

1 5-6 lbs. beef brisket, trimmed of fat
2 bottles of your favorite BBQ sauce
1 medium yellow onion
¼ cup paprika
2 tablespoons chili powder
1 tablespoon ground cumin
1 ½ tablespoons packed brown sugar
1 ½ tablespoons coarse salt
1 ½ teaspoons cayenne pepper
1 ½ teaspoons garlic powder
1 ½ teaspoons black pepper
½ teaspoon celery seed
2-3 tablespoons butter
Hamburger buns

Instructions

Turn on slow-cooker to low, spray with non-stick cooking spray.

Trim brisket and slice in half. Combine paprika, chili powder, cumin, brown sugar, salt, cayenne pepper, garlic powder, celery seed, and black pepper in a bowl and then rub thoroughly into the brisket pieces. Place brisket pieces into slow-cooker.

Pour 1 bottle of BBQ sauce over brisket. Place 2-3 tablespoons of butter in frying pan on medium heat. Brown onions in pan - stirring frequently. Add to slow-cooker mixture.

Cover and cook on low for 9-10 hours.

Remove brisket pieces from slow-cooker and place on cutting board. Discard sauce/liquid in slow-cooker. Slice or shred the brisket pieces and return to slow cooker. Pour second bottle of BBQ sauce over contents. Ready to serve. Alternatively, you can keep the sauce/liquid in the slow-cooker and return the brisket to keep moist (but try to skim out as much fat as you can before returning the brisket pieces). Use second bottle of sauce when serving.

Place on hamburger buns (or serve without buns).

Notes

Serve with potato salad, pickles, and cold beer! If you like the flavor of liquid smoke, you can add ½ to 1 teaspoons to slow-cooker at the beginning of the cooking process.

"NOLA" Gumbo

"A New Orleans specialty, right in your kitchen!"

Ingredients

2 lbs. chicken (breasts, thighs, or combination)

2 lbs. sausage (andouille or chorizo)

1 large yellow onion (diced)

2 - 3 jalapeno peppers (diced, clean out seeds and ribs)

2 celery stalks (diced small)

5 large garlic cloves (minced)

⅓ cup cooking oil

⅓ cup flour

2 bell peppers - one red, one yellow (diced)

4 cups chicken broth/stock

1 tablespoon each of: basil, thyme, oregano, garlic powder, black pepper, and onion powder

1 ½ teaspoons paprika

1 teaspoon salt

1 ½ teaspoons red pepper flakes

2-3 tablespoons butter

White rice

Instructions

Turn on slow-cooker to low, spray with non-stick cooking spray.

Place 2-3 tablespoons of butter in frying pan on medium heat. Brown onions in pan - stirring frequently. When there is about a minute to go, add minced garlic and cook for 1 minute, stirring frequently. Add to slow-cooker. In same pan make a roux: combine cooking oil and flour on low-medium heat. Stir frequently until turns light brown. 15-20 minutes.

While roux is cooking add vegetables to slow-cooker. Slice sausages into discs and cook in different frying pan on medium heat. When brown add to slow cooker. Slice chicken into small pieces and brown in same frying pan. When no pink is visible add to slow cooker.

Pour roux over contents in slow-cooker and add chicken broth/stock.

Add basil, thyme, oregano, garlic powder, black pepper, onion powder, paprika, salt, and red pepper flakes. Stir everything together well. Cover and cook on low for 8 hours.

When ready, serve over white rice (prepared per package instructions).

Notes

You can add just about any left-over meat to gumbo. You can also add okra (sliced, 1 to 1 ½ cups). Serve with corn bread.

Bayou Jambalaya

"Oh me, oh my-o! Big food fun on the Bayou!"

Ingredients

1 ½ lbs. andouille sausage, cut into slices (you can use kielbasa sausage as substitute)
1 ½ lbs. chicken breasts, cut into bite size pieces (you can use chicken thighs or mix both)
1 medium yellow onion (chopped)
5 large garlic cloves (minced)
1 15 oz. can diced tomatoes
1 15 oz. can chicken broth/stock
1 8 oz. can tomato paste
1 yellow or red pepper (seeded, chopped)
2 jalapeno peppers (seeded and diced)
2 celery stalks (chopped)
3 bay leaves
1 ½ cups white rice
½ teaspoon each cayenne pepper, black pepper, creole/Cajun seasoning, salt
1 teaspoon each Tabasco sauce and Worcestershire sauce
2 teaspoons dried basil
1 ½ teaspoons dried oregano
2-3 tablespoons butter
Optional: ½ lbs. shrimp, peeled and deveined (*if* you like seafood)

Instructions

Turn on slow-cooker to low, spray with non-stick cooking spray.
Place 2-3 tablespoons of butter in frying pan on medium heat. Brown onions in pan - stirring frequently. When there is about a minute to go, add minced garlic and cook for 1 minute, stirring frequently. Add to slow-cooker.
Add all of the remaining ingredients other than rice (and optional shrimp). Stir well, cover and cook on low for 4 hours. At around 4 hours, add rice and cook for 1-2 additional hours until rice is tender.
Around 20-30 minutes before serving, add shrimp (if using) and cook for another 20 -30 minutes.

Notes

After you have made this once, adjust spices, vegetables, and seasonings to taste. This is a very flexible recipe. Serve with corn bread and (if desired) extra rice on the side (and, yes, I broke my rule on seafood here – you're welcome).

Chicken Tagine

"Tagine is perfect for the slow-cooker!"

Ingredients

3 lbs. chicken breasts or 8 bone-in/ boneless chicken thighs (whichever you prefer)

2 teaspoons coarse salt

1 teaspoon black pepper

1 large yellow onion (finely chopped) (or two medium onions if you really like onions)

12 cloves garlic (minced)

2 teaspoons ground cumin

1 ½ teaspoons cayenne pepper

1 teaspoon turmeric

½ teaspoon ground ginger

1 ½ teaspoons ground coriander

1 15 oz. can chicken broth/stock

1 cup dried apricots

1 15oz can chickpeas (Garbanzo) (you can add another can if you like chickpeas)

2 cinnamon sticks (3 inch)

2 tablespoons olive oil

2-3 tablespoons of butter

2 lemons (cut into quarters)

White rice or couscous (whichever you prefer)

Instructions

Turn on slow-cooker to low, spray with non-stick cooking spray.

Heat 2 tablespoons of olive oil on medium heat in a large frying pan. Generously salt and pepper the chicken and brown both sides of the meat. Add to slow-cooker. Place lemon wedges around chicken.

Place 2-3 tablespoons of butter in frying pan on medium heat. Brown onions in pan - stirring frequently. When there is about a minute to go, add minced garlic and cook for 1 minute, stirring frequently. Add to slow-cooker.

In same pan add broth, cumin, cayenne pepper, turmeric, ginger, and coriander. Stir together well and raise heat to high and bring to a boil (if you cannot get all the broth/stock in the pan just set aside and add to slow-cooker later). Deglaze the pan (scrape up any brown bits) and add to slow-cooker. Next add the apricots, cinnamon sticks, and chickpeas to slow-cooker.

Cover and cook on low for 5-6 hours. Discard cinnamon sticks before serving. Serve on top of white rice or couscous.

Notes

An optional ingredient is 2 teaspoons of honey. You can also add raisins and green olives if you wish.

Braised Pork Tenderloin

"Good enough for your next dinner party!"

Ingredients

2-3 lbs. boneless pork tenderloin (trimmed of fat)

3 large shallots

2 stalks celery (finely chopped)

5 cloves garlic (minced)

½ teaspoon coarse salt

½ teaspoon pepper

½ cup dry white wine

2 tablespoons white wine vinegar

2 tablespoons olive oil

2-3 tablespoons butter

1 cup chicken broth/stock

Wild rice or egg noodles

Alternative: swap-out white wine and white wine vinegar with dry red wine and red wine vinegar

Instructions

Turn on slow-cooker to low, spray with non-stick cooking spray.

Heat 2 tablespoons of olive oil on medium heat in a large frying pan. Generously salt and pepper the tenderloin and sear both sides of the meat until golden brown on both sides. Add to slow-cooker.

Place 2-3 tablespoons of butter in frying pan on medium heat. Sauté shallots and celery (about 5-6 minutes). When there is about a minute to go, add minced garlic and cook for 1 minute, stirring frequently. Add chicken stock, wine, and vinegar, stir and bring to a boil. Deglaze pan and add mixture to slow-cooker.

Cover and cook on low for 6-8 hours or until pork is very tender.

Serve with wild rice or egg noodles. Skim fat from juices in slow-cooker and use remaining liquid to drizzle on pork.

Notes

Fresh asparagus makes a nice side for this dish. Crusty bread is also a winner.

Lemon Garlic Chicken

"One of my favorites – small effort, big flavors!"

Ingredients

2 ½ lbs. chicken breasts (skinless, bone-less, halves)

10 baby red potatoes (halved or quartered, skins on)

4 tablespoons fresh lemon juice (about 2 medium lemons)

3 cloves garlic (minced)

½ teaspoon coarse salt

½ teaspoon black pepper

⅓ cup chicken broth/stock

1 ½ teaspoons oregano

1 teaspoon rosemary

3 tablespoons butter

Grated parmesan cheese

Instructions

Turn on slow-cooker to low, spray with non-stick cooking spray. Place potatoes on bottom of slow-cooker.

Mix oregano, salt, pepper, and rosemary in bowl. Rub mixture onto chicken pieces. Heat three (3) tablespoons of butter on medium heat in a large frying pan. Brown the chicken breasts (3-5 minutes per side). Add to slow-cooker.

In same frying pan, mix broth/stock, lemon juice, and garlic. Bring to a boil. Pour mixture over chicken in slow-cooker. Cover and cook on low for 6 hours. Remove chicken and potatoes to serve. Garnish with parmesan cheese.

Notes

This is a very versatile dish. You can skip potatoes and serve with pasta or egg noodles. You can add additional vegetables to the mix, e.g., carrots. You can also substitute chicken thighs for chicken breasts. If you like extra lemon flavor, cut up an extra lemon and use slices to add additional juice once served.

Baja Corn Chowder

"Definitely, a soup that's a meal!"

Ingredients

1 ½ lbs. chicken thighs (skinless/boneless, trimmed of fat) (chicken breasts work too)

1 15 oz. can "Mexicorn" (has added red and green peppers). You can use regular corn as well

2 15 oz. cans creamed corn

3 cloves garlic (minced)

1-2 large Russet potatoes (peeled, cut into small cubes)

1 4 oz. can diced green chiles (hot, medium, mild to taste)

2 cups heavy cream

1 cup chicken broth/stock

2 teaspoons chili powder

1 teaspoon paprika

1 ½ teaspoons ground cumin

2 cups of Monterey Jack cheese (freshly grated, if possible)

Salt and pepper (to taste when serving)

Instructions

Turn on slow-cooker to low, spray with non-stick cooking spray. Place potatoes on bottom of slow-cooker.

Add chicken, Mexicorn, creamed corn, garlic, green chiles (undrained), chicken broth/stock, chili powder, paprika, cumin to slow-cooker.

Cover and cook on low for 5-6 hours. When chicken is very tender, remove and shred and return to slow cooker. At this time add heavy cream and Monterey Jack cheese. Stir everything together and serve.

Notes

There are lots of "adds" to this recipe depending on taste. You can add a 15 oz. can of black beans while cooking (and you can remove the potatoes too). You can even swap out cooked chorizo sausage for the chicken. At serving, consider sour cream, avocado, lime, and cilantro. For extra heat, a dash or two of hot sauce goes well with this. And of course, cold Mexican beer is a must!

Zucchini & Squash Soup

"The perfect summer soup!"

Ingredients

1 lbs. zucchini (cut into thin slices or small cubes)

1 lbs. yellow squash (cut into thin slices or small cubes)

2 lbs. ground Italian sausage (hot or sweet.) You can also use sausage links – just slice open and take out the meat

1 small to medium yellow onion (chopped)

3 large cloves garlic (minced)

1 red pepper and 1 yellow pepper (cut into small strips)

2 stalks celery (chopped)

2 28 oz. cans diced tomatoes

2 teaspoons salt

1 teaspoon each of oregano, Italian seasoning, dried basil, and white sugar

2-3 tablespoons butter

Grated parmesan cheese (to garnish soup)

Croutons (optional)

Instructions

Turn on slow-cooker to low, spray with non-stick cooking spray.

Place 2-3 tablespoons of butter in frying pan on medium heat. Brown onions in pan - stirring frequently. Add sausage and celery and cook until celery is soft (8-10 minutes). When there is about a minute to go, add minced garlic and cook for 1 minute, stirring frequently. Drain any grease and add mixture to slow-cooker.

Add zucchini, squash, pepper, tomatoes (with liquid), salt, oregano, Italian seasoning, dried basil, and sugar.

Cover and cook on low for 5-6 hours. Serve and garnish with parmesan cheese and croutons.

Notes

This is an excellent soup. You can adjust the ingredients to taste and you can add other/different vegetables. Serve with crusty bread.

Texas Style BBQ Chicken

"God bless Texas for this recipe!"

Ingredients

2 — 2 ½ lbs. skinless, boneless chicken breasts

2 bottles of BBQ sauce (18 oz. each). Just pick your favorite.

2 teaspoons red pepper flakes

1 ½ teaspoons garlic powder

¼ cup brown sugar

¼ cup distilled white vinegar

Optional: 1 small yellow onion (sliced into circles)

Instructions

Turn on slow-cooker to low, spray with non-stick cooking spray.

Place chicken breasts on bottom of slow-cooker.

In a bowl, mix 1 bottle of BBQ sauce, red pepper flakes, garlic powder, brown sugar, and white vinegar. Stir well, until everything is mixed, and brown sugar has dissolved. Pour on top of chicken.

Toss onion slices on top of chicken (if using).

Cover and cook on low for 6 hours. You can leave chicken breasts whole or shred before serving.

Serve with extra BBQ sauce if needed.

Notes

Serve with beans and favorite buns. Potato chips go great with this. If serving on buns, dill pickle slices add a nice, tart flavor. Same with coleslaw. Corn on the cobb is a must.

Pork Loin with Apples

"Pork and apples – best friends!"

Ingredients

3.5 to 4 lbs. pork loin

2 apples (Granny Smith or Honey Crisp), sliced

1 medium yellow onion (chopped)

½ teaspoon each of salt, pepper, and dried thyme

1 teaspoon cinnamon

½ cup honey

2-3 tablespoons of butter (for onions)

8 tablespoons of butter (for loin)

Wild rice (cooked per instructions)

Instructions

Turn on slow-cooker to low, spray with non-stick cooking spray. Slice up 8 tablespoons of butter and place on bottom of slow-cooker.

Place 2-3 tablespoons of butter in frying pan on medium heat. Brown onions in pan - stirring frequently. Add to slow-cooker.

Cut slits in the pork loin (about 1 ½ inches apart and 1 to 1 ½ inches deep depending on depth of the loin). Plug apple slices into each slit. Place pork loin in slow-cooker on top of onions and butter.

In a small bowl mix the salt, pepper, cinnamon, and thyme. Sprinkle over pork loin.

Drizzle honey over pork loin. Cover and cook on low for 6-7 hours.

Serve on bed of wild rice.

Notes

You can pick your favorite apples to use. If you really like cinnamon (which is a strong spice) you can kick it up a notch and use up to a tablespoon – but would go easy the first time you make this as you can always sprinkle more cinnamon on pork loin when serving. Egg noodles can replace wild rice.

Ratatouille & Sausage

"I can't pronounce it, but I love it!"

Ingredients

4-6 large smoked sausages (Polish, etc.)

3 large yellow onions (chopped)

6 large cloves garlic (sliced thin)

8 Plum tomatoes (seeded, then cut into chunks)

1 red pepper and 1 yellow pepper (seeded then cut into chunks)

2 medium eggplants (trimmed and cut into chunks)

1 zucchini and 1 yellow squash (cut into chunks)

1 cup chicken broth/stock

2 tablespoons tomato paste

1 teaspoon salt

½ teaspoon black pepper

1 teaspoon dried thyme

½ teaspoon dried oregano

2 bay leaves

3 tablespoons olive oil

3 tablespoons butter

Instructions

Turn on slow-cooker to low, spray with non-stick cooking spray.

Place 3 tablespoons of butter in frying pan on medium heat. Brown onions in pan - stirring frequently. With about a minute to go, add garlic and sauté for about 1 minute. Add to slow-cooker. Add chicken broth/stock.

Place tomatoes, peppers, eggplant, zucchini, and squash in slow-cooker. Whisk olive oil, tomato paste, salt and pepper together in small bowl. When mixed well, add to slow-cooker.

Add thyme, oregano, and bay leaves. Mix into vegetables well. Cover and cook on low for 5 hours. At 5-hour mark, remove cover and let some of the liquid evaporate and reduce. You want moist, but not a soup. Approximately 60 minutes.

During the evaporation period, looking to the time when you want to eat, prepare your sausages. Make several small slits in each sausage and cook in a frying pan on medium heat. Cook until done and brown on all sides. When serving, you can serve whole or cut into pieces to mix with the ratatouille.

Notes

You can substitute just about any vegetable you have around the house (or just add more from the list above). You can also substitute chicken for the sausage. Serve with crusty bread. Topping with parmesan cheese is a flavorful idea too.

Cuban Ropa Vieja Stew

"Wow! This will be your new favorite!"

Ingredients

2 lbs. sirloin steak (you can also use stew meat or flank steak) (cut into small pieces)

1 medium white onion (chopped)

6 -8 cloves of garlic (crushed)

1 15 oz. can of diced tomatoes (no salt)

3 cups beef broth/stock

2 teaspoons coarse salt

1 teaspoon black pepper

3 ½ teaspoons cumin

2 teaspoons Mexican oregano

1 teaspoon of red wine vinegar or apple cider vinegar (your preference)

1 yellow bell pepper (seeded and chopped)

1 red bell pepper (seeded and chopped)

Fist full of cilantro (chopped)

2 tablespoons olive oil

3 tablespoons butter

Optional: 1 cup Spanish olives

Instructions

Turn on slow-cooker to low, spray with non-stick cooking spray.

Heat olive oil in large frying pan – high/medium heat. Brown meat in pan (you may have to cook in batches). Transfer meat and juices to slow-cooker. Add beef broth/stock.

Place 3 tablespoons of butter in frying pan on medium heat. Brown onions in pan - stirring frequently. When you think you have about a minute left to brown onions, add the crushed garlic. Cook for a minute then add onions and garlic to slow-cooker on top of meat.

Add tomatoes, Mexican oregano, cumin, vinegar, yellow bell pepper, red bell pepper, olives (if using), salt, and pepper. Stir everything together well. Cover and cook on low for 6-8 hours until meat is very tender.

Serve with a lot of cilantro on top.

Notes

Serve with yellow, white, or Spanish rice. Black beans make a nice addition too. You can even heat up some corn or flour tortillas and use the ropa vieja as a filling. Like many things made in the slow-cooker, this dish will taste even better the next day as the flavors seep in together overnight in refrigerator.

Ham & Lentil Soup

"Everyone will love this hearty soup!"

Ingredients

2 cups dried lentils

½ lbs. smoked ham (cubed) (or use 1 large ham hock or cut up two smoked pork chops)

2 tablespoons crumbled bacon

3 cloves garlic (minced)

1 small yellow onion (chopped)

½ cup celery (diced)

½ cup carrots (diced)

4 15 oz. cans chicken broth/stock (with one extra can to use if needed during cooking)

1 15 oz. can diced or crushed tomatoes (no salt added, drained)

1 ½ teaspoons black pepper

1 teaspoon dried oregano

2 tablespoons red wine vinegar

3 tablespoons of butter

Instructions

Turn on slow-cooker to low, spray with non-stick cooking spray.

Add lentils and chicken stock/broth.

Place 3 tablespoons of butter in frying pan on medium heat. Brown onions in pan - stirring frequently. When you think you have about a minute left to brown onions, add the garlic. Cook for a minute then add onions and garlic to slow-cooker.

Add bacon, celery, carrots, salt, pepper, oregano. Cover and cook on low for 8 hours.

With about one hour left, add the tomatoes and vinegar. If you use a ham hock, make sure meat has shredded from bone. If not, remove shred and return the meat to slow-cooker. Add broth/stock if needed during cooking.

Notes

You can make this without the bacon and ham (if so, add 2 teaspoons of salt). Or you can substitute sausage for ham (cook the sausage before adding). If you like a thicker soup, you can leave the lid off for the last hour and let it cook down. This soup will taste even better the next day, so prepare a day in advance and let sit overnight in the refrigerator. Serve with crusty bread.

Bolognese Sauce

"Tastes like your favorite Italian restaurant!"

Ingredients

2 lbs. ground beef

2 lbs. ground pork

2 cups red wine

1 cup whole milk

3 teaspoons coarse salt

1 teaspoon black pepper

4 tablespoons butter

2 onions (large) chopped

4 celery stalks, finely chopped

2 carrots finely chopped

8 large garlic cloves, minced

4 15 oz. cans diced/crushed tomatoes

1 6 oz. can tomato paste

1 tablespoon oregano

1 tablespoon basil

2 teaspoons thyme

2-3 teaspoons red pepper flakes

½ teaspoon nutmeg

2 lbs. spaghetti (or fettuccine or angel hair pasta)

Parmesan cheese (grated)

2 bay leaves

Instructions

Turn on slow-cooker to low, spray with non-stick cooking spray.

Place 4 tablespoons of butter in frying pan on medium heat. Brown onions in pan - stirring frequently. When you think you have about a minute left to brown onions, add the garlic. Cook for a minute then add celery, carrots, oregano, basil, and thyme. Cook until they begin to soften (about 4-6 minutes). Then add mixture to slow-cooker.

In stock pot or Dutch oven, add ground beef and pork (you may have to cook meat in two batches). Brown the meat over medium heat, stirring frequently. When cooked through, add tomatoes, wine, milk, salt, black pepper, nutmeg, and red pepper flakes. Stir together well and cook for 4 minutes. Add to the slow-cooker with bay leaves and stir.

Cover slow-cooker and cook on low for 6 hours. When close to ready, cook the pasta per directions. Place pasta in bowl, serve. Pour sauce over pasta and top with lots of freshly grated parmesan cheese.

Notes

Serve with a crusty bread and salad. Experiment to get the right combination of garlic and onions to suit your family.

Chicken Quinoa Stew

"Super healthy, super flavorful!"

Ingredients

4-5 boneless chicken breasts

4 large cloves garlic (minced)

1 medium yellow onion (chopped)

32 oz. chicken stock/broth

1 15 oz. can diced tomatoes

1 cup uncooked quinoa

8 oz. Portabella mushrooms (chopped)

2 teaspoons curry powder

2 teaspoons dried oregano

2 bay leaves

5 green onions (chopped)

1 ½ teaspoons black pepper

2 large yellow potatoes (diced)

2 stalks celery (diced)

3 tablespoons butter

Instructions

Turn on slow-cooker to low, spray with non-stick cooking spray.

Place 3 tablespoons of butter in frying pan on medium heat. Brown onions in pan - stirring frequently. When you think you have about a minute left to brown onions, add the garlic. Cook about one minute.

While onions are cooking, place raw chicken breasts on bottom of the slow-cooker.

Pour onion/garlic mixture over the chicken. Add all remaining ingredients. Stir together well. Cover the slow-cooker and cook on low for 7-8 hours. Use extra broth if needed during cooking.

When ready, toss bay leaves and remove chicken. Shred chicken with fork and return to slow-cooker. Mix together well and serve.

Notes

Serve with crusty bread or cornbread. You can also substitute the yellow potatoes with sweet potatoes for a sweeter taste (or add a handful of dried apricots).

Italian Wedding Soup

"A wedding of ingredients from the old country!"

Ingredients

1½ lbs. of pre-prepared Italian-style meatballs (in grocer's freezer section)

1 large yellow onion (finely diced)

1 ½ cups carrots (chopped)

¾ cups celery (sliced)

9 cups chicken broth/stock

1 ½ tablespoons Italian seasoning (or 1 tablespoon parsley and 1 teaspoon oregano)

¾ cup elbow pasta (or Acini di Pepe or pastina)

3 cups spinach leaves or escarole (washed and coarsely shredded)

¼ teaspoon coarse salt

¼ teaspoon black pepper

3 tbsp. butter

7 cloves garlic (minced)

Grated or shredded parmesan cheese (or other hard Italian cheese)

Instructions

Turn on slow-cooker to low, spray with non-stick cooking spray.

Place 3 tablespoons of butter in frying pan on medium heat. Brown onions in pan - stirring frequently. When you think you have about a minute left to brown onions, add the garlic. Cook about one minute. Pour mixture into slow-cooker. Add meatballs to slow-cooker (still frozen is okay). Add the remaining ingredients – except for the pasta and spinach/escarole. Cover and cook on low for 8 hours. Add uncooked pasta and spinach/escarole and cook on high for another 30 minutes to 1 hour (until pasta is tender). Serve with cheese and garlic bread (or plain crusty bread).

Notes

Another great recipe to add other ingredients you might have around the house, like cauliflower or other vegetables. Also, play around with ratios and amounts to get just the right flavor for your family. If meatballs are "large," you can cut into smaller pieces before adding. You can also chop, shred, or mince everything to different sizes – whatever you prefer.

Chicken Marsala

"Wine, mustard, and chicken all come together!"

Ingredients

4-5 lbs. chicken breasts (you can also use thighs or a whole chicken cut into parts)

½ cup Marsala wine

½ cup Chardonnay wine (or other dry white wine)

¾ cup diced shallots

1 cup chicken broth/stock

3 ½ tablespoons Dijon mustard (can use other spicy mustard if needed)

1 ½ teaspoons ground mustard

1 teaspoon sugar

2 ½ tablespoons flour

2 bay leaves

2 teaspoons coarse salt

5 sprigs fresh thyme

1 teaspoon black pepper

¼ cup balsamic vinegar

3 tablespoons butter

3 large cloves garlic (minced)

2 tablespoons bacon bits (optional)

Instructions

Turn on slow-cooker to low, spray with non-stick cooking spray.

Salt the chicken pieces.

Melt butter in frying pan over medium-high heat. Brown chicken on both sides. You will likely need to brown in two batches. Place chicken in slow-cooker and cover.

In same skillet, add shallots and garlic. Reduce heat to medium. You may need to add an extra tablespoon of butter. Cook for 60 seconds then add wine, vinegar, thyme, bay leaves. Bring to boil and add chicken broth/stock. Stir well. Cook for one minute then add mustard and sugar and bring to a boil. Once boiling, remove from stove and pour over chicken in slow-cooker.

Cover and cook on low for 6 hours. Remove chicken to a platter and cover. Add flour to juices in slow-cooker and cook on high for 15-20 minutes. Serve chicken with the sauce.

Notes

Serve with egg noodles, thin pasta, rice, or couscous. French bread is a nice side for this dish. As is chocolate pudding.

Sausage Casserole

"Meat and potatoes? You got it!"

Ingredients

2 -2 ½ lbs. smoked sausage (diced). You can use kielbasa, andouille, chorizo, or any type of pre-cooked sausage. You can also use uncooked sausage (Italian, bratwurst, etc.) so long as you cook it first.

2 lbs. baby potatoes (cut into chunks). Skins on or off to preference. You can use any kind of potato, just cut into chunks (peel or not is up to you)

1 large yellow onion (diced)

3 large cloves garlic (minced)

3 stalks of celery (chopped)

1 teaspoons Creole/Cajun seasoning

8 oz. Portabella mushrooms (chopped)

3 cups chicken broth/stock

3 tablespoons butter

2 tablespoons Worcestershire sauce

Feta cheese

Instructions

Turn on slow-cooker to low, spray with non-stick cooking spray.

Place 3 tablespoons of butter in frying pan on medium heat. Brown onions in pan - stirring frequently. When you think you have about a minute left to brown onions, add the garlic. Cook about one minute. Pour mixture into slow-cooker.

Add sausage, potatoes, celery, mushrooms, chicken broth/stock, Worcestershire sauce, and Cajun seasoning to slow-cooker. Stir well.

Cover and cook on low for 8 hours.

Top with Feta cheese.

Notes

Another recipe where you can alter the ingredients and amounts with little risk of disaster. It's a casserole, so pretty much anything goes. You can use any type of cheese to top it with, e.g., Blue Cheese crumbles are interesting. And, of course, a little crusty bread always goes nicely.

Azorean Spiced Beef

"Thank you, Portugal! Thank you!"

Ingredients

2-2 ½ lbs. stew beef or chuck roast cut into small pieces

12 large cloves garlic (minced)

1 large yellow onion (diced)

2 stalks celery (chopped)

2 carrots (shredded)

1 tablespoon tomato paste

2 cups white wine (you can substitute chicken broth/stock)

1 teaspoons cumin

1 teaspoon all-spice

1 tablespoon red pepper flakes

2 ½ tablespoons coarse salt

1 bay leaf

1 cinnamon stick

3 tablespoons butter

Instructions

In a large bowl use your hands to mix the beef, ½ of the minced garlic, red pepper flakes, and salt. Coat the meat well then cover the bowl and let sit in refrigerator for 4 hours (or longer if you wish).

When ready to cook, turn on slow-cooker to low, spray with non-stick cooking spray. Place 3 tablespoons of butter in frying pan on medium heat. Brown onions in pan - stirring frequently. When you think you have about a minute left to brown onions, add the garlic. Cook about one minute. Pour mixture into slow-cooker. Add beef to slow-cooker then add all of the remaining ingredients. Mix together well. Cover and cook on low for 8 hours or until meat is very tender.

When ready, discard cinnamon stick and serve.

Notes

Serve over buttered egg noodles or white rice. You can also add baby red potatoes to the slow-cooker. If so, quarter the potatoes and add an extra ½ cup of white wine or chicken stock/broth. After you have made it once, adjust spices to taste.

Spicy Big Game Chili

"Chili was meant for slow-cookers!"

Ingredients

2 lbs. ground beef

1 lbs. sausage (hot Italian, chorizo, or other sausage to taste). Sausage can be ground or, if links, slit open casing and remove the meat

5 large cloves of garlic (minced)

1 large red onion (chopped)

4 tablespoons chili powder

1 tablespoon cumin

1 cup beer (or beef broth)

2-3 chipotle chilies in adobo sauce (chopped)

1 teaspoon coriander

2 15 oz. cans diced tomatoes

2 15 oz. cans kidney beans (rinsed and drained)

2 15 oz. cans tomato sauce

1 4 oz. can diced green chilies (optional)

1 teaspoon coarse salt

1 teaspoon black pepper

3 tablespoons butter

1 teaspoon white sugar

Grated extra sharp cheddar cheese

Instructions

Turn on slow-cooker to low, spray with non-stick cooking spray.

Brown ground beef and sausage together in frying pan on medium heat. When browned, drain and add to slow-cooker. Place 3 tablespoons of butter in frying pan on medium heat. Brown onions in pan - stirring frequently. When you think you have about a minute left to brown onions, add the garlic. Cook about one minute. Pour mixture into slow-cooker over meat.

Add all remaining ingredients, stir well to combine. Cover and cook on low for 8 hours. Taste and add additional seasonings (chili powder, salt, pepper, etc. as desired).

Notes

Serve with corn bread. Top with grated cheese and sour cream. Extra chopped onion and cilantro is nice too. Add broken corn chips or tortilla chips for extra flavor and texture. Chili is a "kitchen sink" recipe, so feel free to add or subtract ingredients, or change amounts to suit your taste.

Beer Braised Short Ribs

"Beer is nature's wonder ingredient!"

Ingredients

5 lbs. beef short ribs

2 medium size yellow onions (chopped)

5 large cloves of garlic (minced)

2 stalks celery (chopped)

8 oz. Portabella mushrooms (sliced)

15 baby carrots (more or less to taste)

1 large butternut squash (peeled, seeded, cut into large pieces)

1 lbs. zucchini (cut into slices)

1 15 oz. can diced tomatoes (with juice)

1 bottle dark beer (Guinness or dark Mexican beer)

3 tablespoons flour

Montreal steak seasoning mix

Instructions

Turn on slow-cooker to low, spray with non-stick cooking spray.

Generously season the short ribs with Montreal steak seasoning. Place on a broiler pan and brown under broiler (3-4 minutes per side). Alternatively, you can use a grill at medium-high heat and brown both sides of the short ribs. Place the ribs in slow-cooker.

Place 3 tablespoons of butter in frying pan on medium heat. Brown onions in pan - stirring frequently. When you think you have about a minute left to brown onions, add the garlic. Cook about one minute. Pour mixture into slow-cooker over ribs.

Add remaining ingredients (except for flour). Cover slow-cooker and cook on low for 8 hours (or until meat is easily separating from the bones and zucchini and squash are tender).

When ready, remove ribs and vegetables from slow-cooker with a slotted-spoon, place in a large bowl or platter and cover with foil. Mix flour with small amount of water and then add to juices in slow-cooker. Mix together and turn slow-cooker to high. Stir frequently and let sauce thicken (about 10-15 minutes). When serving, spoon sauce over the ribs and vegetables.

Notes

Since you probably have at least 5 bottles of dark beer left, serve those with the ribs! Otherwise, there are so many great ingredients here, there is not much of a need to serve anything else with it.

Chicken Cordon Bleu

"Straight from France and into your slow-cooker!"

Ingredients

5 boneless chicken breasts

5 thin slices of Black Forest Ham (or any ham from grocery store deli)

5 slices Swiss cheese

1 can cream of chicken or cream of mushroom soup (to your preference)

8 oz. chicken broth/stock

4 tbsp. olive oil (or vegetable oil)

Grated parmesan cheese

Instructions

Turn on slow-cooker to low, spray with non-stick cooking spray.

Using two pieces of wax paper, place a chicken breast between paper and pound to about ¼ inch thickness. Repeat for remaining chicken breasts.

Lay chicken breasts flat and place 1 slice of ham and 1 slice of Swiss cheese on each. Roll up and secure with toothpicks or twine.

Heat oil in large frying pan on medium-high heat. Brown the rolled-up chicken breasts on all sides. Remove from frying pan and place in slow-cooker.

Pour soup and chicken broth/stock over the rolled-up chicken breasts. Cover the slow-cooker and cook on low for 5 hours. Chicken needs to be tender and fully cooked (i.e., at least 165 degrees F).

Garnish with parmesan cheese when serving.

Notes

Serve with noodles, pasta, or white rice. Warm bread and butter is nice too. A spinach salad goes very well with this dish. Also, I know I said that I don't like to use canned soup for anything but need to make an exception here.

Madurai Butter Chicken

"The first bite is amazing!"

Ingredients

3 lbs. chicken thighs (boneless, skinless) cut into small pieces (you can use chicken breasts too)
1 large yellow onion (diced)
2 shallots (finely chopped)
3 tablespoons grated ginger
6 large cloves garlic (minced)
2 teaspoons chili-powder
2 tablespoons garam masla (similar to French Herbes de Provence or Chinese five-spice and you can find it online if you cannot buy at grocery store)
1 teaspoon lemon juice
1 teaspoon lime juice
Zest of two limes
1 can coconut milk (14 oz.)
1 cup plain Greek yogurt
1 can tomato paste (6 oz.)
1 teaspoons cayenne pepper
1 teaspoons cumin
1 teaspoons turmeric
½ cup chicken broth
1 teaspoon coarse salt
3 tablespoons butter
2 tablespoons olive oil
Naan (flat bread) for serving
Jasmine or basmati rice for serving

Instructions

Turn on slow-cooker to low, spray with non-stick cooking spray.

Place 3 tablespoons of butter in frying pan on medium heat. Brown onions and shallots in pan - stirring frequently. When brown, add ginger and garlic and cook for 60 seconds, then add salt, garam masla, cumin, turmeric, tomato paste and cook for 90 seconds – stirring frequently. Place mixture in slow-cooker. Using the same frying pan, add olive oil and then brown the chicken on all sides. When ready, add to slow-cooker. Add all remaining ingredients (except yogurt, naan, and rice, which are for serving later). Stir everything together well, cover and cook on low for 6 hours. With 30 minutes to go, stir in yogurt.

Serve with rice and naan.

Notes

This is an amazing dish that tastes buttery, even though no butter is used other than to brown the onions. As usual, the spices used and amounts can vary to your taste.

Potato & Cauliflower Soup

"Sounds weird, but taste's so good!"

Ingredients

6 medium potatoes (peeled and cut into cubes)

1 head of cauliflower (cut into florets)

1 large onion (chopped)

2 stalks celery (chopped)

2 carrots (peeled & diced)

5 cloves garlic (minced)

6 cups chicken broth/stock

¼ teaspoon cayenne pepper

1 teaspoon coarse salt

1 teaspoon ground black pepper

1 cup half-and-half

3 tablespoons butter

Instructions

Turn on slow-cooker to low, spray with non-stick cooking spray.

Place 3 tablespoons of butter in frying pan on medium heat. Brown onions in pan - stirring frequently. When brown, add garlic and cook for 60 seconds – stirring frequently. Place mixture in slow-cooker.

Add potatoes, celery, carrots, cayenne pepper, salt, black pepper, and chicken broth/stock. Stir together well, cover and cook on low for 6 hours.

Uncover and place soup into blender and blend until smooth (you can also use an immersion blender directly in the slow-cooker). You will have to blend in batches. When smooth return soup to slow-cooker.

Add half-and-half and stir, blending everything together. Let soup heat back up (about 10-15 minutes) and it's ready to serve.

Notes

You can also add chunks of ham to this soup (or any pre-cooked meat). Top the soup with bacon crumbles and/or shredded cheese (Monterey Jack, sharp cheddar, etc.). Chunks of crusty bread are the perfect garnish.

Lonestar Chili

"My go to dish for any big game party!"

Ingredients

3 lbs. stew meat (or chili meat/ground beef)
6 tablespoons chili powder
1 yellow onion (chopped)
4 cloves garlic (minced)
½ cup Hungarian sweet paprika
1 tablespoon Tabasco sauce
2 tablespoons ground cumin
1 tablespoon cayenne pepper
2 cans tomato sauce (15 oz. ea.)
2 teaspoons oregano
3 tablespoons olive oil
½ white onion (chopped, for garnish)

Instructions

Turn on slow-cooker to low, spray with non-stick cooking spray.

Place 3 tbsp. oil in frying pan and heat to medium heat. Add beef and brown on all sides (you may have to brown in batches). Place in slow-cooker with juices.

Add all of the remaining ingredients, stirring well together. Cover and cook on low for 7 hours. Taste and adjust seasonings. Cover and let cook for 1 more hour. You may need to add some liquid throughout the cooking process. If so, use more tomato sauce or beef broth/stock.

Notes

This is a dish best made the night before serving. Let it sit in refrigerator overnight. Before warming back up in the slow-cooker (on low), skim off the fat and discard. Serve with shredded sharp cheddar cheese, diced tomatoes, and oyster crackers. Cornbread is the perfect side.

Dry Rub Ribs

"Amazingly tender and spicy – and so easy!"

Ingredients

4-5 lbs. ribs (beef or pork). If using pork, remove the membrane from back – use a paper towel for grip

Make dry rub – combine in bowl

    2 tablespoons garlic powder

    2 tablespoons coarse salt

    2 tablespoons black pepper

    1 tablespoon paprika

1 large yellow onion, sliced

2-3 lemons juiced

Instructions

Cut ribs into portions that will fit inside slow-cooker. Rinse and pat dry. With a heavy sprinkle, cover ribs with mix. Cover and place ribs in refrigerator for up to four hours.

When ready, pre-heat oven broiler. Turn on slow-cooker to low, spray with non-stick cooking spray.

Brown ribs under the broiler. Put ribs on broiler pan and place about 6 inches under broiler. Cook for about 10 minutes (or until brown), flipping once.

When browned, put ribs into slow-cooker. Sprinkle extra rub on top. Place onions in slow-cooker, cover ribs. Squeeze lemons so juice gets on top of the ribs.

Cover and cook for 7-10 hours – until ribs are your desired tenderness. Beef ribs usually take a bit longer than pork ribs.

Notes

If you don't want dry ribs, you can simply add a cup or two of your favorite BBQ sauce on top of the ribs before they start to cook. Serve with corn on the cob and beans. You can skip the lemon if not to taste, the meat will be ridiculously tender regardless. You can also use store bought dry rub or create your own. Finally, you don't have to brown the ribs – but you will be glad you did!

Beef Stroganoff

"Takes a little work, but everyone will love it!"

Ingredients

2 — 2½ lbs. stew meat (or use sirloin steak sliced into thin strips)

10 oz. fresh mushrooms (cleaned, sliced)

1 ½ cups beef broth/stock

1 yellow onion (chopped)

2 teaspoons Italian seasoning

3 tablespoons Worcestershire sauce

4 cloves garlic (minced)

2 ½ tablespoons Dijon mustard

¾ tablespoon thyme

2 teaspoons coarse salt

1 ½ teaspoons ground black pepper

1 cup sour cream

6 oz. cream cheese (cut into cubes)

3 tablespoons cornstarch (dissolved in ½ cup beef broth/stock)

1 large package egg noodles (prepared per instructions)

3 tablespoons butter

1 tablespoon olive oil

Instructions

Turn on slow-cooker to low, spray with non-stick cooking spray.

Place 3 tablespoons of butter in frying pan on medium heat. Brown onions in pan - stirring frequently. When brown, add garlic and cook for 60 seconds — stirring frequently. Place mixture in slow-cooker.

Add oil to same frying pan, heat, then add beef and brown on all sides. Add to slow-cooker.

In a large bowl, combine broth/stock, Italian seasoning, Worcestershire sauce, Dijon mustard, thyme, salt, and pepper. Mix well and pour into slow-cooker. Add mushrooms.

Cover and cook on low for 8 hours.

About 30 minutes before done, add corn starch. Stir everything well. Add cream cheese and sour cream, stir, then cook another 20-30 minutes until cream cheese and sour cream are well incorporated and sauce thickens.

When ready, serve over hot egg noodles (prepared per package instructions).

Notes

Another recipe where you will likely need to adjust seasonings and quantities to taste.

Creamy Tortellini Soup

"I couldn't believe a soup could taste this good!"

Ingredients

1 ½ lbs. sweet Italian sausage (open casings and remove ground sausage)

1 16 oz. package of refrigerated cheese tortellini

½ of a yellow onion (chopped)

5 large cloves garlic (minced)

¾ lbs. fresh mushrooms (cleaned and sliced)

2 16 oz. cans whole peeled tomatoes

1 cup dry red wine

5 cups beef broth/stock

1 teaspoon dried basil

1 teaspoon dried oregano

8 oz. cream cheese (cubed)

3 tablespoons butter

1 tablespoon olive oil

Instructions

Turn on slow-cooker to low, spray with non-stick cooking spray.

Place 3 tablespoons of butter in frying pan on medium heat. Brown onions in pan - stirring frequently. When brown, add garlic and cook for 60 seconds – stirring frequently. Place mixture in slow-cooker.

Add oil to same frying pan, heat, then add Italian sausage and brown. Drain and add to slow-cooker.

Add mushrooms, peeled tomatoes, wine, beef broth/stock, basil, oregano, and cream cheese to slow-cooker. Cover and cook on low for 7 hours.

Add tortellini and stir well – make sure soup has a smooth consistency. Cook for 30 additional minutes.

Notes

Serve with grated romano cheese (to top soup) and garlic bread.

Slow-Cooker Lasagna

"Yes, you can make lasagna in your slow-cooker!"

Ingredients

1 lbs. ground beef

1 lbs. ground Italian sausage

6 large cloves garlic (minced)

1 teaspoon Italian seasoning

2 teaspoons dried oregano

1 teaspoon dried basil

1 teaspoon coarse salt

1 teaspoon black pepper

1½ teaspoons garlic powder

1 cup romano (sharp) cheese

2 cups shredded mozzarella

1 package frozen cheese ravioli (25 oz. bag)

2 jars (24 oz. each) prepared marinara sauce (or red sauce you prefer)

Directions

Turn on slow-cooker to low, spray with non-stick cooking spray.

In a large frying pan, brown the ground beef and Italian sausage. Drain and place on plate with paper towel to soak up extra grease.

In a bowl, pour the red sauce. Then add garlic, garlic powder, Italian seasoning, oregano, basil, salt, pepper, and romano cheese. Stir together well. Add ground beef and Italian sausage. Stir well.

Ladle a good amount of the sauce combination onto the bottom of the slow cooker. Then add a layer of ravioli. Cover with a good amount of sauce. Add another layer of ravioli and alternate until all the sauce and ravioli are used.

Cover and cook on low for 5 hours. Uncover and add the mozzarella cheese. Cover and cook for another hour (or until the cheese is well melted).

Notes

Serve with a salad and garlic bread. Sprinkle top with romano or parmesan cheese.

Dakdoritang Chicken

"Powerful flavors from the Far East!"

Ingredients

2½ lbs. chicken (mix boneless thighs and breasts, cut into small pieces)

5 medium size potatoes (peeled and cut into medium cubes)

1 large yellow onion (chopped)

3 large carrots (cut into small chunks)

6 cloves garlic (minced)

3 tablespoons Korean chili paste (Gochujang)

2 tablespoons Korean chili flakes (Gochugaru)

4 tablespoons soy sauce

2 tablespoons rice wine (or mirin)

1 tablespoon honey

1 tablespoon sesame oil

½ teaspoon ginger powder

½ teaspoon black pepper

1 teaspoon raw sugar

½ cup chicken broth/stock

3 tablespoons butter

Jasmine rice (prepared per instructions for serving)

2 tablespoons sesame seeds (for garnish)

3 stalks green onion (thinly sliced for garnish)

Instructions

Prepare marinade sauce by combining chili paste, chili flakes, soy sauce, rice wine/mirin, honey, sesame oil, pepper, ginger, and sugar in a large bowl.

Add the chicken and stir well. Cover the bowl with plastic wrap and let marinade in refrigerator overnight (you can skip the over-night marinade if you want, but the flavor is much better if you let it sit). When ready to cook, turn on slow-cooker to low, spray with non-stick cooking spray. Place 3 tablespoons of butter in frying pan on medium heat. Brown onions in pan - stirring frequently. When brown, add garlic and cook for 60 seconds – stirring frequently.

While onions are cooking, layer the potatoes and carrots on the bottom of the slow-cooker. Then, pour the chicken and marinade sauce over the top. Add chicken broth. When ready, pour the onion and garlic mixture on top. Cover and cook on low for 6 hours.

When cooked, skim fat. Then serve over rice in bowls. Garnish with sesame seeds and green onions.

Notes

You can order Korean chili paste and flakes online. You can also experiment with amount of chili paste and flakes to taste, as well as using "large" chunks of the vegetables. If you prefer, use large chunks of onion and add without browning.

Pork Stew with Apples

"Together again, and so good!"

Ingredients

4 lbs. boneless pork shoulder (trimmed of fat and cut into 2 inch or bigger pieces)

5 large green apples (peel and core, cut into chunks)

2 medium white onions (chopped)

4 large cloves smashed garlic

3 teaspoons red pepper flakes

1 teaspoon cayenne pepper

Coarse salt

Black pepper

5 cups chicken broth/stock

3 bay leaves

¼ teaspoon ground cloves

⅓ cup fresh lime juice

½ cup sour cream

¼ cup chopped cilantro

White rice for serving (prepared per instructions)

1 tbsp. olive oil

3 tbsp. butter

Instructions

Turn on slow-cooker to low, spray with non-stick cooking spray.

Generously salt and pepper the pork and then in large skillet, over high-medium heat, add oil and – when hot - brown the pork on all sides. You may have to brown in batches. When done, add pork to slow-cooker.

In same skillet, add butter and then sauté the onions, apples, garlic, cloves, pepper flakes, and bay leaves. About 10 minutes. You may need to cook in batches. When ready, pour over pork in slow-cooker. Add chicken broth/stock and then add cayenne pepper and lime juice. Stir together well.

Cover and cook on low for 6-8 hours. When close to ready, prepare rice for serving per instructions. In a blender or food processor, combine cilantro and sour cream and blend until very smooth. Serve stew over rice and use cilantro/sour cream blend as a drizzle over the stew.

Notes

This is an old Peruvian recipe adapted for a slow-cooker. You will need to adjust seasonings per your family's taste (hotter, milder, more/less onions, etc.). Use any apples handy. You can also add other vegetables like potatoes, mushrooms, etc. It's all good! You can substitute pork loin for shoulder (less fat) and you do not need to cut into small chunks, you can use several large pieces of pork and then shred with forks before serving. Finally, while not authentic, naan flatbread is fantastic with this stew..

Pernil Adobo Pork

"If heaven has a smell, it smells like this!"

Ingredients

8 lbs. pork shoulder roast (bone-in with skin removed, but with nice layer of fat on one side)

18 large cloves garlic

2 tablespoons coarse salt

1 tablespoon black pepper

2 tablespoons ground cumin

¼ cup olive oil

1 ½ tablespoons dried oregano

2 tablespoons distilled white vinegar

1 large yellow onion (quartered)

White rice (prepared per instructions)

Instructions

The roast needs to marinate <u>24 hours</u>, so plan ahead.

Combine garlic, salt, pepper, cumin, olive oil, oregano, vinegar, and onion in blender or food processor. Blend to a thick paste. You *do not* want to liquefy the paste so blend for a few seconds at a time.

Take roast and cut a bunch of slits on all sides (you will work the paste into these slits).

Rub paste with hands all over the roast. Be sure to work it into the slits. Place the roast – fat side down- into the slow-cooker insert. Cover tight with plastic wrap and place in refrigerator to marinade over night.

When roast has marinated, place insert into slow-cooker, turn on low, and cook for at least 10 hours. When ready, the bone will easily detach, and the meat will shred easily.

Remove roast from slow-cooker and place on cutting board, toss the bone, and shred with two forks. Serve with white rice.

Notes

If heaven has a smell, it smells like this Puerto Rican pork roast! You can also get by with marinating for an hour or two, but it will *not* have the same depth of flavor. If you have the time, let it marinate for 48 hours. The meat will freeze well and can be used for sandwiches and tacos.

Carole's Red Sauce with Meat Balls

"My mother Carole's classic red sauce and meatballs. This will make you a hero!"

Ingredients

2 lbs. pasta (spaghetti, penne, fettucine, whatever you like).

Sauce Ingredients
6 large cloves garlic (peeled/minced)

1 28 oz. can crushed tomatoes (buy the top shelf brand at your store)

1 6 oz. can tomato paste (buy the top shelf brand)

1 tablespoon coarse salt

½ tablespoon ground black pepper

⅛ cup oregano

⅛ cup garlic powder (not garlic salt)

⅛ cup dried basil leaf

1 teaspoon white sugar

½ cup grated parmesan cheese (get the good stuff)

1 cup grated romano cheese (get the good stuff)

1 tablespoon olive oil

5 Italian sausages

Meatball Ingredients
7 large cloves garlic (peeled and minced)

1 lb. ground beef (80/20)

½ tablespoon coarse salt

½ teaspoon ground black pepper

1 tablespoon garlic powder

2 eggs

1 cup romano cheese

¼ cup dried parsely flakes

½ cups bread

crumbs

Olive oil

Instructions

Turn on slow-cooker to low, spray with non-stick cooking spray.

Place "sauce" olive oil in a large stock pot on stove. Use low-medium heat. When oil is hot, place the "sauce" minced garlic (6 cloves) and cook until glistening (a few minutes).

Add the can of crushed tomatoes. Fill the empty can *halfway* full of tap water and add that to the pot. Then add the tomato paste. Fill that empty can *full* of tap water and add to the pot. Stir together well and keep on low heat.

In a small bowl, add the "sauce" salt, pepper, oregano, garlic powder, basil leaf, and sugar. Mix together well and add to the stock pot. Then add the "sauce" romano and parmesan cheese amounts. Stir contents of stock pot together well.

Carefully, pour contents of stock-pot into the slow-cooker. Cover and cook on low for at least 6 hours.

While sauce is cooking, brown the Italian sausages in a frying pan on stove. Poke holes in sausages to allow better draining. Drain on a paper towel covered plate. When drained, cut the sausages into chunks and place in the slow-cooker with the sauce.

To make the meatballs, put all of the "meatball" ingredients from above into a large mixing bowl. Use your hands to *thoroughly* mix all of the ingredients together. When ready, form meatballs with hands – make them golf-ball size or smaller. Place on a platter or cookie sheet.

Add olive oil to large frying pan. You want to fully cover the pan as you will be searing the meatballs in the oil (just cover the surface with oil – you're not frying the meatballs). Use medium heat. When oil is hot, add meatballs. You will need to brown in bunches. Sear/brown the meatballs on *all* sides. You do not want any raw meat in the slow-cooker. Turn frequently and don't let a hard crust develop. When ready, place seared/browned meatballs on a paper towel covered-platter to drain. Cook the remaining meatballs until finished. When all of the meatballs have properly drained, slowly add to the slow-cooker to cook for the remaining 6 hours.

When ready, serve with cooked pasta and extra romano and parmesan cheese.

Notes

This is a recipe that has been passed-down from my Italian grandmother to my mom to me. Whenever I make it, it reminds me of my mother's kitchen or her visits to our house in Texas. You will likely have to adjust the garlic to the level your family prefers. Serve with garlic bread or plain crusty bread. This makes excellent meatball/sausage sandwiches too. And it freezes well. If you have a large group, just double the recipe (but you will need two slow-cookers).

CPSIA information can be obtained
at www.ICGtesting.com
Printed in the USA
LVHW070627191218
601015LV00025B/2233/P

9 781545 645376